OUTDOOR NORDIC COOKING

Bjarne Larsen

www.bjarnelarsen.com

FSC
www.fsc.org
MIX
Papir fra
ansvarlige kilder
Paper from
responsible sources
FSC® C105338

OUTDOOR NORDIC COOKING

BJARNE LARSEN

PHOTO: BJARNE LARSEN

www.bjarnelarsen.com

First published in 2016

Copyright Bjarne Larsen

Forlag: BoD-Books on Demand, København, Danmark
Fremstilling: BoD - Books on Demand GmbH - Norderstedt, Tyskland

ISBN: 978-87-7691-554-4

CONTENTS

Foreword

Outdoor cooking is a wonderful activity for families. It is not even necessary to go camping—it can all take place in your garden! This book guides you through ways to build pizza ovens with clay and stones, outdoor stoves, and a variety of campfires with different purposes.

The recipes in this book are easy to prepare and include pizzas, burgers, twist bread, grilled sausages, potato fries, and more.

The book is for everyone who is looking for new ideas and inspiration. Invite your neighbors, friends, and family over and start the fire!

Campfire safety:

- When setting up a fire, make sure that the location is safe and clear of flammable vegetation such as long grass.
- Never leave your fire unattended. Children and pets should be supervised by an adult.
- Keep a bucket of water or a fire extinguisher nearby.

Campfires

Always use dry wood when building a fire. Wet or moist wood will burn poorly and create a lot of unnecessary smoke and pollution. Avoid adding more wood to the fire than needed and do not add plastic and/or painted wood to the fire. Also, avoid particleboard as it contains glue. Smoke from painted wood can be toxic and the smell is rather unpleasant.

Wooden spit for Twist Bread

Bamboo spit are great for twist bread. Other spit can be used as well, as long as the bark has been removed at the end where the dough will be. Make sure that this part of the stick is clean before twisting the dough.

Campfire Safety

Equipment for extinguishing a fire should always be available when cooking outdoors.
Follow these rules and check your local area for other guidelines:

1. Never set up a fire in places where it is at risk of spreading.
2. Do not add gasoline or other flammable liquids that might result in explosions.
3. Make sure the fire is extinguished completely before you leave it.
4. Do not leave the fire unattended and make sure that children and pets are supervised.

In case the grass catches fire, use a fire swatter to extinguish the flames with sweeping movements.
A fire extinguisher with foam or chemicals is also useful to keep in the vicinity of the fire place.

If using a bucket of water to terminate the fire, do not empty it all at once. With your hands, shovel the water to kill the fire; not much

water is needed. Sand and soil are also useful for smothering a fire. When preparing food over fire, avoid using too much grease and oil, as it can catch on fire. If a fire ignites in a pot, have a lid ready and put it on to stop the fire and, if possible, remove the pot from the campfire.

If the grease on a stone is on fire, let it burn out.

Pouring water on a grease fire will not put it out. The oil will pop and splatter and if people are too close it can result in burns on the skin. A fire blanket will be a useful item to put out grease fires if they haven't spread too far.

In the event of a campfire being out of control, alert the emergency services.

Location
When placing a campfire, it is important to choose a location where the fire is not at risk of spreading. Take into consideration that the smoke should not bother neighbors.

Digging out a Fire Pit
The fireplace should be at least 1 x 1 meter (3 x 3 feet) so there is plenty of space around the fire. Use a shovel to dig the foundation. If the fire pit is on a lawn, the sections of turf that are being dug out can be put back in place when you are done with the fire. Remember to water them.

The Edge
To prevent the fire from spreading, encircle the fire pit with rocks. Avoid using rocks that are likely to explode when heated.

From time to time, the outdoor cooking equipment may be in need of a little repair work here and there.

Build a Campfire with Flagstones

This fireplace on the terrace is made of regular flagstones glued together with flagstone glue.

Apply the glue with a wolf's tooth spatula to gain an even layer of glue. Build up the fireplace as in the photo. Use a mallet to make sure the stones are in place and wipe off excessive glue with a moist cloth.

Cast Iron Pot

These are available at most home and garden supply shops. By placing a grill on top, this is the perfect barbecue. Do not use a grill made of galvanized steel as this material is toxic.

Types of Campfires

When cooking outside, there are various kinds of campfires that can be used, depending on the food being prepared.

Ember Fire

When using pots or pans for cooking, small flames in the fire pit are just fine. However, when cooking *in* the fire, such as twist bread or sausages, there should be no flames as the food will be burned.

Teepee Fire

Place the tinder in the middle and surround it with smaller twigs. Place larger sticks around in the shape of a teepee

Platform Fire

Often used when cooking with pots and pans. Start with a teepee fire as described above, and put two larger logs on each side for the pot to rest on. Make sure the logs are stable.

Stone Fireplace
Useful for cooking
with pots and pans.
Surround a teepee
fire with three stones
on which to place a
pot or a pan.

Star Fire
Can be used as a campfire and for
cooking with pots. Start with a
teepee fire in the middle and place
four to eight larger logs in the
shape of a star. As they burn, push
them further in toward the middle.
This fire can be
used with
hanging pots.
Build a tripod by
connecting
three long, thick
sticks at least
one meter in
length. In the
middle, place a
bent stick on
which to hang
the pot.

Working Table
Good to have for food preparation.

Food Storage
Make sure to wrap food and always keep dairy and meat in a cool place.

Hygiene
Good hygiene is vital when cooking. Always make sure that utensils, pots, and pans are washed and clean. Wash your hands prior to cooking and avoid leaving food on the ground and on unclean surfaces.
Also, do not forget to bring a bag and pack your trash.

Homemade Refrigerator
If a fridge is not available, food can stay cold in a cement pipe by keeping it moist.
A box covered with a moist cloth is useful to store food. As the water evaporates, the food will stay cool. Make sure to place the box in the shade and not in the sun.

Vegetables
Rinse well and keep away from raw meat to avoid cross contamination.

Weeds
When cooking with weeds, make sure they are edible and, if in doubt, do not eat them. Also, avoid picking them from areas where weed killer might have been sprayed. Do not pick weeds near freeways and train tracks due to exhaust gases.

Meat
Make sure meat is cooked thoroughly before serving in order to avoid food poisoning.

Build a Pizza Oven with Cement
Materials:
Sand or gravel (must be moist)
1 flat stone 10-15 cm. (4-6 inch) in thickness. This is for the bottom; the pizza will be baked on it.

Wet newspapers
Cement
Perlite
Wire
Tiles and bricks for the foundation
Start by building a foundation with tiles and bricks, and make sure it is level. Put the stone in the bottom, and place the moist sand/gravel on the stone and build up a cone-shaped top. The height should be 60 cm. and the diameter 60 cm. (2 feet).

To protect the sand/ gravel, put a layer of wet newspapers on top of it.

Mix the cement and the perlite (1 part cement, 3,5 parts perlite). Add a little water and mix well.

Apply the concrete and smooth it with a trowel. Cover the cone with 5 centimeters (2 inches) of concrete. On the top, make a chimney.

It is necessary to control the thickness by pressing a screwdriver into the newspapers. Once the concrete is firm, place a wire net on top to ensure the shape. Finally, apply another 10 centimeters (4 inch) of concrete and let it dry before smoothing the surface with a wood float. Let the oven dry for a couple of days. Empty it of sand/gravel and do not use it until it is completely dry.

When it is dry, light a fire inside the oven and let it burn for a couple of hours. Once it has burned out, clean the insides with a brush. Again, light a fire and let it burn out. When the stone is hot, scrape the burning coals toward the sides, so they can keep heat.

Clean the ashes and coal from the stone and the oven is now ready for its first pizza.

Build a Pizza Oven with Clay
The procedure is nearly the same as building a pizza oven with mortar.

Materials needed:
Large stones for the foundation
50-80 kilograms clay (100-160 lbs).
Sand to mix with the clay
Hay to mix with the clay
1 flat stone with a thickness of 10-15 cm (4-6 inches) (this stone will be in the bottom of the oven and will be used to bake the pizzas on)

Since this oven requires a lot of clay, it is advisable to find and dig it up from the ground.

To raise the pizza oven above the ground, build a foundation of stones about the same size as handballs. Fill the space between the stones with soil and press lightly.
Place the flat stone in the bottom. Top it with moist sand/gravel and shape up a dome. The height should be 60 cm. (2 feet) and the diameter 60 cm. (2 feet).
To protect the sand/gravel, cover the dome with moist newspapers.

The clay on the dome should be mixed with sand to make it stronger. Mix 1 part sand with 5 parts clay.
A fun and easy way to knead sand and clay is to pour the sand over the clay. If the clay is dry, add a little water. Turn on the music and ask your family to join you for a barefooted dance until the sand and clay are well mixed.
Put 10 cm. (4 inches) clay on the dome. On the top, make a hole for a chimney.

When the first layer has been applied, ask your family for another dance—this time including the hay. Mixing hay with clay will help isolate the oven. When this has been mixed well, apply another layer of clay 15 cm. (6 inches).

When the clay is dry, cut a hole for the opening and smooth the edge. Build up a chimney around the hole you made for that purpose.
Use a moist sponge to smooth out the surface.
Let the oven dry for a couple of days and remove the sand/gravel with a little shovel.
When the oven is dry, light a fire in its front. The embers should be pushed back little by little.

Before use, it is recommended to clean the inside of the oven with a brush. Once clean, light a new fire and let it burn for a couple of hours. When the stone is hot, push the embers to the sides so it will stay hot. The oven is ready for use when it is free of embers and ashes.
It is advisable to cover the oven in case of rain. If the surface cracks, another layer of clay can be applied.

Pizza Preparation

There are several ways to bake a pizza. Use a stone, a lid, or a frying pan.

Pizza baked on a stone: Find a large, flat stone and light a fire around it. Once the stone is hot, brush it and place the pizza on it. Bake it until the edges are brown.

Pizza baked on a frying pan on a tripod of stones:

3 large stones
1 frying pan
Place the stones near each other and light a fire in the middle. Place the pan on top and, when hot, bake the pizza until the edge has reached a light brown color.

Pizza baked in a lid

1 metal lid
Foil
Butter or margarine
Clean the lid and cover the bottom with foil. Place a thin layer of pizza dough in the lid and let it rise for 15 minutes. Add the toppings and place the lid in the embers and let the pizza bake until the dough is brown.

Baking Time

The baking time will vary between 20 and 35 minutes. It all depends on the method being used.
The dough will swell as the pizza is being baked, so a thin, flat base is preferable.

All recipes are for four people

Pizza Dough with Yeast

25 grams compressed yeast (cake yeast) (1,5 tbsp).
2.5 deciliters lukewarm water (1 cup).
300 grams wheat flour (10,5 oz).
100 grams whole-wheat flour (5,5 oz).
1 tbsp. oil
1 tsp. salt

Pour the water and the oil into a mixing bowl and dissolve the yeast in it. Add salt.
Add the whole-wheat flour and most of the wheat flour and mix with a spoon. Knead the dough thoroughly. If it is too sticky, add more flour.
Let it rise for 30 minutes

Pizza Dough with Baking Powder

When yeast is replaced with baking powder, the result will be a crisper base.

3.5 tsp. of baking powder
1.5 deciliters milk (0,63 cup).
400 grams all-purpose flour (14 oz).
90 grams of butter (3 oz).
1 tsp. salt

Mix the flour with salt and baking powder and knead it with the butter. Heat the milk and knead everything together.

If the dough is too sticky, add a little more flour.

Pizza Sauce
1 onion
1-2 cloves of garlic
2 tbsp. oil
400 grams of chopped tomatoes
(14 oz).
4 tbsp. tomato puree
2 tsp. dried oregano
1 tsp. salt
Pepper
1 tsp. sugar

Peel and chop the onion and the
garlic. Heat the oil in a pot, add
onion and garlic. Sauté lightly and
mix with all of the other
ingredients. Let the sauce cook
until you like the consistency.

**Pizza with Squash, Onion,
and Cheese**
1 portion pizza dough
1 portion pizza sauce
1 large onion
200 grams squash (7 oz).
2-3 tbsp. oil
1 tsp. salt
2 tsp. dried rosemary
200 grams grated cheese—
any kind (7 oz).

Peel the onion and slice it
thinly. Remove the seeds
from the squash and cut it

into small cubes.
Sauté the onion and the squash in
oil for a couple of minutes. Add
salt, pepper, rosemary then mix.
Roll out the pizza dough in suitable
sizes and spread the pizza sauce.
Top with the sautéed vegetables
and cheese.
Bake until the crust has reached a
light brown color.

Pizza with Mushrooms

1 portion pizza dough
1 portion pizza sauce
2 tbsp. oil
200 grams mushrooms (7 0z).
100 grams squash (3,5 oz).
1 green pepper
1 onion
1 tsp. salt
2 tsp. dried oregano
200 grams feta cheese (7oz).

Slice the onion, the mushrooms, and the pepper and sauté them in oil for a couple of minutes. Add salt and oregano.
Roll out the pizza dough and add the sauce. Top it with the vegetables and feta cheese. Bake until the crust is brown.

Pizza with Onion, Tomatoes, and Cheese

1 portion pizza dough
2 onions
4 tomatoes
2-3 tbsp oil
1 tsp. salt and pepper
20 olives
2 tsp. thyme
200 grams grated cheese—any kind (7oz).

Peel the onions and slice them along with the tomatoes. Sauté the onions for a couple of minutes and add salt and pepper.
Roll out the pizza dough in suitable sizes and sprinkle with onions, tomatoes, olives, thyme, and cheese.
Bake until the edge of the crust is brown.

Pizza with Ground Beef, Tomatoes, and Cheese

1 portion pizza dough
2 cans of chopped tomatoes
2 tsp. of oregano
1 tsp. salt
A little flour
400 grams of ground beef (14 oz)
200 grams of grated cheese—your choice (7 oz)

Drain the canned, chopped tomatoes, pour them into a mixing bowl and add the salt and oregano. Mix with a spoon and add flour until you like the consistency.

Sauté the ground beef in a pan for a couple of minutes and mix with the other ingredients.

Roll out the pizza dough in suitable sizes and spread with the tomato and ground-beef sauce. Sprinkle with cheese and bake until the edge of the crust is brown.

Pizza with Ground Beef and Cheese

1 portion pizza dough
2 green peppers
200 grams mushrooms

Pizza sauce:
400 grams ground beef (14 oz)
200 grams grated cheese (7 oz)
2-3 tbsp. oil

Slice the peppers and the mushrooms. Roll out the pizza dough and spread the pizza sauce. Fry the ground beef for a couple of minutes and add it to the pizzas with the vegetables. Sprinkle with cheese.

Clay Stove
Materials:

1 large portion clay
Sand
A flat stone

To strengthen the clay, mix in sand (see page 19). Once the clay and the sand have been mixed, knead it together and roll out a couple of thick coils. Place the coils on top of each other and smooth the surface.

On the front, make an entrance and, on the back, coil up the clay. This stove can be made with an open fire place and thereby used for pots and pans (Page 27). Alternatively, a flat stone can be placed for the purpose of meat preparation. On the top edge, make a fold for the stone. The clay must not reach the stone, since the clay will retract when it dries which will lead to cracks.

Build the chimney by placing coils of clay on top of each other, making the coils shorter toward the top. Smooth and shape as you wish.

When the texture of the clay is leather-like, smooth it with a moist sponge. The clay needs to dry slowly. If the air is very dry, place a cloth and some plastic on top. When the clay is finally dry, light a little fire in the stove. This fire needs to burn for a couple of hours before using the stove. If the stove is made of clay, a pot or pan should not be placed too hard on the stove, since the clay isn't burned yet.

In case of rain, cover up the stove. Cracks can be fixed by adding a new layer of clay.

Stove Built of Flagstones and Mortar
Flagstones
Clay pipe
Cement
Mortar
Water

Another way to build a stove is to use flagstones, a drain pipe, cement, and mortar. Mix the cement and the mortar.

Place the flagstones like the ones in the photo and make an opening on top to place the pot or the pan. The chimney is a pipe made of clay or cement.
Cover the stones with a layer of mortar and make sure it is dry before using the stove.

Apply soft soap to the outside of the pot to make cleaning the pot easier.

Stove

The procedure is the same except from a hole where the pan or pot is placed upon.

If the stove is made of clay, be careful when you set a pot or a pan on it.

Burger Buns
6 deciliters water (2,5 cups)
50 grams compressed yeast (3 tbsp)
4 tbsp. oil
2 tsp. salt
2 tsp. sugar
1 kilogram all-purpose flour (2 lbs)

Heat the water until lukewarm. Dissolve the yeast in the warm water and add the remaining ingredients and most of the flour. Knead thoroughly. If the dough is too sticky, add more flour. Knead the dough, place a cloth over it, and let is rise for 45 minutes.

Whole-Wheat Burger Buns
6 deciliters milk (2,5 cups)
50 grams compressed yeast (3 tbsp)
4 tbsp. oil
2 tsp. sugar
2 tsp. salt
400 grams cottage cheese (14 oz)
300 grams whole-wheat flour (10,5 oz)
700 grams wheat flour (1,5 lbs)

Same procedure as above.

Burger Buns Baked in a Saucer
4 saucers
Margerine
4 portions of dough

These buns will be prepared in the embers. An easy and quick way to bake these breads is to use a saucer. Clean the saucer and coat the inside with margarine. When the dough has risen, place it in the saucer and let it rise again for 15 minutes.

Place the saucer in the embers and let it bake until the bread is brown around the edges, 15-20 minutes. When the bread has cooled off a bit, it is ready to be served and can easily be taken from the saucer. If the bread is charred, scrape it off.

Burgers
480 grams ground beef (1 lbs)
Oil
Salt
Pepper
Dressing
Mustard
Ketchup
Fried onions
4 burger buns

Shape the ground-beef patties and add salt and pepper. Put oil on the hot stone and fry the burgers on both sides until they are cooked enough.
Slice the buns and apply mustard and ketchup on the bottom bun, add meat, dressing, and the fried onions. Lastly, add the top bun.

Burgers with Bacon
480 grams ground beef (1 lbs)
Oil
Salt
Pepper
Mustard
Ketchup
Dressing
4 tbsp. garlic herb butter
8 pieces of bacon
4 burger buns

Same procedure as the burger on previous page, except that in this recipe you fold a disc of garlic herb butter into the center of the burger. As it grills, the butter melts keeping the meat moist even when cooked through.

Burgers with Beech Leaves
480 grams ground beef (1 lbs)
Oil
Salt
Pepper
2 avocados
4-5 tbsp. sour cream
1 tbsp. lemon zest
3 deciliters fresh beech leaves (1 cup)
4 burger buns

Shape the patties and season with salt and pepper. Oil the stone and fry the burgers on both sides until cooked through.
Cut the avocados and scoop out the meat. Mash the avocado meat with a fork and mix with sour cream and lemon zest.
Rinse the beech leaves and chop them.
Part the buns and brush them with dressing and sprinkle the chopped beech leaves on top. Add the meat and assemble the burger.

Burger with Chili
480 grams ground beef (1lbs)
½ tsp. dry chili
1 tsp. oregano
1 tsp. paprika
1 egg
1 large onion
2 cloves of garlic
A little cream

Oil
Salt
Pepper
Lettuce
Tomatoes
1 cucumber
Dressing
4 slices of cheese
4 burger buns

Peel and chop the onion and the garlic. Mix the chopped onion and garlic with the ground beef and the spices.
Rinse the lettuce, tomatoes, and the cucumber and slice them.
Form the patties and season with salt and pepper. Brush the stone with oil and fry patties on both sides until cooked through. Just before the patties are cooked, add a slice of cheese and let it melt.
Cut the buns in half and brush with mustard and ketchup. Assemble the burgers with lettuce, meat with cheese, cucumbers, and tomatoes.

Spicy Burgers

480 grams ground beef (1 lbs)
Oil
100 grams carrots (3,5 oz)
1 onion
50 grams oatmeal (2 oz)
1 tsp. dried thyme
1 tsp. dried basil
Salt
Pepper
Lettuce
1 cucumber
Tomatoes
Dressing
4 burger buns

Peel the carrots and grate them with a shredder. Peel the onion and chop it.

Blend the ground beef with carrots, onion, basil, thyme, and oatmeal. If it feels too dry, add milk.

Form the patties and season with salt and pepper. Rinse the lettuce and the tomatoes and slice the latter.

Brush some oil on the stone and fry the patties thoroughly on each side. Spread the dressing on the bottom bun. Assemble the burger with lettuce, meat, cucumbers, and tomatoes and the top bun.

Potato Burgers

600 grams potatoes (1,3 lbs)
2 deciliters water
4 eggs
Salt and pepper
4 tbsp. wholegrain flour
Mustard
Ketchup
Crisp onions
Lettuce
4 burger buns

Peel and boil the potatoes. Drain the water and mash the potatoes with a fork. Mix the mashed potatoes with the remaining ingredients and shape the burgers. Fry on both sides.

Slice the buns and build the burger with lettuce, condiments, and crisp onions as you like.

Chickpea Burgers
480 grams chickpeas
(1 lbs)
2 cloves of garlic
1 large onion
4 tbsp. wheat flour
½ deciliter lemon
juice (0,4 cups)
1 egg
Flour for breading
Oil for frying
 Condiments:
Dressing
Mustard
Ketchup
4 burger buns

Beet Burgers
4 deciliters beets (1,6 cups)
1.5 deciliters carrots (0,6 cups)
75 grams oatmeal (6 oz)
1 onion
2 cloves of garlic
2 eggs
1 tbsp. oil for frying
Salt and pepper
Lettuce
4 burger buns

Soak the chickpeas for 10-12 hours.
Throw away the water and mash
the chickpeas; a food processer can
be used. Peel and grate the onion
and the garlic. Add remaining
ingredients and mix well. Bread the
burgers with flour and fry on both
sides.
Halve the buns and place the
burgers. Top with condiments and
serve.

Condiments: Mustard, Ketchup

Peel and grate the beets, carrots,
and onions and place them in a
bowl. Add the remaining
ingredients and mix it. If it is too
moist, add more oatmeal

Form the patties and fry on both
sides.
Halve the buns, build the burgers,
and serve.

Fried Potato Wedges

1 bag of frozen potato
wedges
2 sieves
1 stick
Wire

Put some potatoes in a
sieve (not too many).
Place another sieve on
top and connect them
with wire. Place the
sieves close to the
embers and turn slowly.
It is a good idea to place
the sieves on a stick as
shown in the photo.
This will take 30-40
minutes.

Twist Bread

Use a stick of 1.5 meter (5 feet) length and peel off the bark at the thinnest end where the dough will be. Make sure this end is clean. Roll the dough into a coil and twist it around the top end of the stick and make sure it stays in place.

When baking, keep the bread close to the embers but not so close that it will char. Also, keep the bread away from flames.

Turn the bread slowly and take it away from the embers when it has reached a golden color and is no longer sticky.
Be cautious—the bread can be hot. Serve with jam.

Dough for Twist Bread

6 deciliters water (2,5 cups)
50 grams compressed yeast (3 tbsp)
2 tsp. salt
2 tsp. sugar
3 tbsp. oil
1 kilogram all-purpose flour (2,4 lbs)

4 sticks

Dissolve the yeast in lukewarm water and add the remaining ingredients. Knead the dough thoroughly and, if it sticks too much, add more flour. Put the dough in a bowl and cover with a kitchen towel. Let it rise for 30 minutes.

Alternatively, use 200 grams (7 oz) of whole-wheat flour and 800 grams (1,7 lbs) of wheat flour.

Cocoa Twist Bread

6 deciliters water (2,5 cups)
50 grams compressed yeast (3 tbsp)
2 tsp. salt
3 tbsp. oil
900 grams wheat flour (1,9 lbs)
100 grams cocoa (3,5 oz)
4 sticks

Same procedure as regular twist bread.

Twist Bread with Ham

400 grams ham (14 oz)
1 portion dough for twist bread

Slice the ham into little cubes and knead into the dough.

Twist Bread with Ham and Cheese

4-8 slices of cheese
8 slices of ham
1 portion dough for twist bread

Hold the cheese near the stick and fold the ham around it. Roll the dough into a thin coil and twist it around the cheese and ham.

Whole-Grain Twist Bread with Flaxseeds

6 deciliters lukewarm water (2,5 cups)
50 grams compressed yeast (3 tbsp)
2 tsp. salt
3 tbsp. oil
100 grams flaxseeds (3,5 oz)
200 grams graham flour (7 oz)
700 grams wheat flour (1,5 lbs)

4 sticks

Same procedure as twist bread.

Twist Bread with Apples
4 apples
1 portion twist bread dough
Butter
Cinnamon sugar

4 sticks

Cut the apples into quarters and
remove the seeds. Hold an apple
close to the stick and wrap the
dough around it.
Once baked, brush with
melted butter and sprinkle with
cinnamon sugar.
Return the bread close
enough to the fire for a moment to
make
the sugar melt.

Barbecue Sausages

What is a barbecue without sausages? These sausages can be grilled in the embers or over a campfire.

Grilled Sausages

4 Sausages

Condiments:
Mustard
Ketchup
Relish
Crisp onions

4 breads (twist breads are fine for this purpose)
4 sticks

Put a sausage on a stick and grill it over the embers while turning slowly until it is cooked through.

Hotdogs
4 sausages
1 portion dough for twist bread

Condiments:
Mustard
Ketchup
Cucumber relish
Crisp onions

4 sticks

Put a sausage on a stick and wrap
the dough around it. Hold it over
the embers and turn the stick
slowly. When the bread has a light
brown color, remove the stick and
cut the bread lengthwise and put
condiments in the opening.

Grilled Sausages with Bacon

4 sausages
8 slices of bacon

Condiments
Mustard
Ketchup
Relish
Crisp onions

4 pieces of bread
4 sticks
Cotton

Put a sausage on a stick and wrap bacon around it. If it doesn't stick, secure it with cotton.

Stuffed Sausages Wrapped in Bacon

4 sausages
2 onions
8 slices of bacon
Foil

Condiments
Mustard
Ketchup

Slit the sausages lengthwise. Peel and chop the onions. Press the chopped onion into the ridges in the sausages and wrap bacon around. Wrap in foil and place the packages in the embers for 10-15 minutes.

Ember Roasted Sausages
4 sausages
2 onions
4 tomatoes
Butter

Mustard
Ketchup

Bread

1 foil tray
Foil

Across the sausages, cut some slits. Peel the onions and slice them and the tomatoes thinly. Press these slices into the slits.
Put some butter in the foil tray with

the sausages and cover it with foil. Leave it in the
hot embers for 15 to 20 minutes.

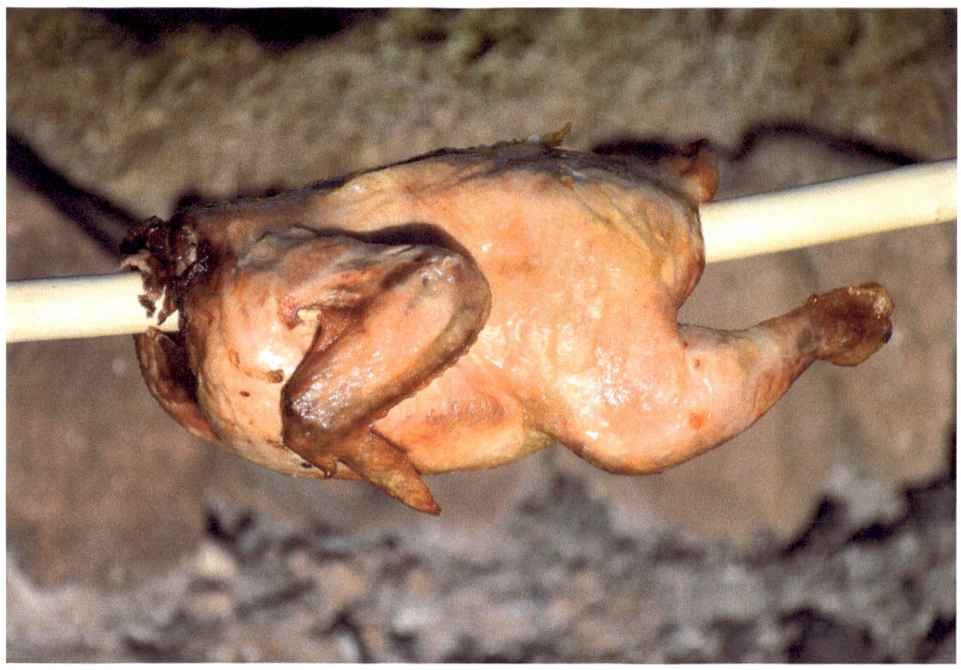

Grilling on Sticks

Nearly all types of meat can be used for grilling on sticks. For larger pieces of meat, metal skewers are more useful than wooden ones. Grilling time for larger sized meats is 1 hour per 10 cm (4 inch) of meat in diameter.

Brush the meat with vegetable oil regularly while grilling to avoid dryness. Season with spices as you like.

Grilled Chicken

Cleanse the chickens well. If the chickens are frozen, be aware that heart and kidneys can we wrapped in plastic inside the chicken.

It is important to cook chickens thoroughly, which means the meat should not be red. When the meat is white and loose, the chicken is ready to be served.

Chicken on a Stick

2 chickens
Vegetable oil
Salt
Cotton yarn
Sticks

Press the stick through the chickens and tie the thighs with the yarn. Rub the chickens with salt and brush with vegetable oil.
In order for the stick to be stable, place two solid forked sticks at each end of the campfire to support the stick with the chicken.
The chickens should be 45 cm (2 feet) above the coals. Turn the chickens regularly to grill evenly. Grill time: 2 hours.

Chicken in Clay

2 chickens
Clay
Foil

Rinse the chickens and cover them in wet clay to a thickness of 2 - 2,5cm (1 inch) (feathers on the chickens are just fine).
Place the chickens in the fire and cover with coals. Grilling time is 1-1½ hours. The meat should be white and loose. When the clay is removed, the feathers will follow. If the chickens have no feathers, it may be helpful to wrap them in foil before wrapping the clay around them.

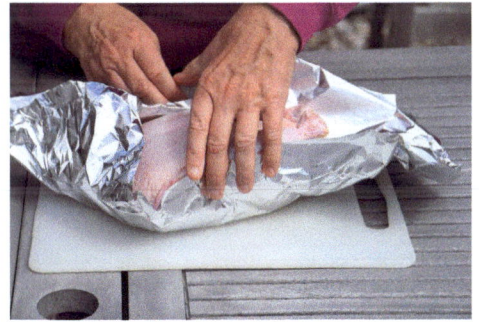

Shawarma with a Pipe

1 pipe (height: 30 cm, diameter: 30 cm) (12 inch) The material must not be flammable

Dig a hole 30 cm in depth and 80 cm in diameter (12 inch 32 inch). Surround it with rocks and place the pipe in the middle of the hole. Make a tripod of three sticks to hang the skewer on. It should be bent at one end to prevent the meat from falling off.

Hang the skewer with wire so that it is suspended within the pipe. Since coals surround the pipe, it isn't necessary to turn the stick. Grill for 20-30 minutes.

Shawarma with 3 Boards
3 boards of a
noncombustible material
Foil
Large rocks
3 Sticks
Wire

Cover the boards with foil
and make sure to turn the
foil's shiny side outward
so the heat from the fire
will be reflected. Place
the boards against some
rocks and place the rest
of the rocks in a half
circle in front of the
boards.

Tie the skewer to the
tripod with wire and turn
it. Grill for 20 to 30
minutes.

Kebab

The kebab is cooked over the embers until the meat is well done. Turn the skewer to make sure it is grilled evenly.

Skewers

480 grams beef (1 lbs)
4 potatoes
2 onions
4 apples
8 small tomatoes
Vegetable oil
4 metal skewers

Cut the meat in cubes. Peel the onions. Peel the potatoes and cut them into cubes. Peel the apples and slice them.
Stick the cubes and the slices on the skewers and brush with oil.

Turkey Kebab

120 grams beef cut in cubes (4 oz)
120 grams turkey cut in cubes (4 oz)
8 slices of bacon
4 sausages
1 green pepper
2 onions
8 small tomatoes
4 metal skewers

Rinse the vegetables and cut them in similar-sized pieces. Slice the sausages and put everything on the skewers.

Vegetable Kebab

120 grams mushrooms (4 oz)
1 small squash
1 green pepper
2 onions
8 small tomatoes
Vegetable oil
4 metal skewers

Rinse and slice the squash, pepper, and onion and thread them onto the skewers. Brush with oil.

When the mushrooms are brown and the tomatoes crack, the kebab is ready
to be served.

Grilled Fish on a Plank

4 flounder filets
4 wooden planks
12 wooden pegs

Rinse the fish, cut it along the back, and remove the bones. Fasten the filets to the wood with the pegs. Use a knife to cut holes for the pegs. The skin of the fish should be placed against the wood. When the fish is fastened to the wood, place it on the embers.
When the meat is white and loose, the flounders are ready to be served.

Grilled Fish in Dough

4 fish
2 onions
100 grams mushrooms
Butter
Salt
Pepper
1 portion dough

Rinse the fish. Peel the onions. Rinse the mushrooms and cut them into cubes. Do the same with the onions. Stuff the fish with the vegetables and wrap dough around them about 2,5 cm. (1 inch). Place these packages in the embers and grill for 15 to 20 minutes.

The dish is ready to be served when the meat is white and coming loose.

Fish in Foil

4 fish
2 onions
Butter
Salt
Pepper

Peel and chop the onions. Season the fish with salt and pepper and wrap them and the onions in foil along with the butter. Place in the embers and grill for 15 to 20 minutes.

Fish in a Wet Newspaper

4 fish
2 onions
Butter
Salt and pepper

4 wet newspapers
Parchment paper

Rinse the fishes. Peel and chop the onions. Stuff each fish with onions and add butter. Season with salt and pepper. Wrap each fish in parchment paper and a wet newspaper and place them in the embers. Grill for 15 to 20 minutes. If the newspaper catches fire, splash it with water.

The dish is ready when the meat is white and loose.

OUTDOOR NORDIC COOKING

BJARNE LARSEN

www.bjarnelarsen.com